DANCE!

Emma McFarland
Illustrated by Kate Sutton

Houghton Mifflin Harcourt.

Dance! was originally published in English in 2016.
This edition is published by arrangement with Oxford University Press.

U.S. Edition copyright © 2019 by Houghton Mifflin Harcourt Publishing Company
Text and illustrations © Oxford University Press 2016

All rights reserved. No part of this work may be reproduced or transmitted in any form or by any means, electronic or mechanical, including photocopying or recording, or by any information storage or retrieval system, without the prior written permission of the original copyright owner identified herein, unless such copying is expressly permitted by federal copyright law.

Printed in China

ISBN 978-0-358-26310-4

1 2 3 4 5 6 7 8 9 10   XXXX   28 27 26 25 24 23 22 21 20 19

4500000000   A B C D E F G

Acknowledgments

Series Editor: Greg Foot
Inside illustrations by Kate Sutton

The publisher would like to thank the following for the permission to reproduce photographs: **Cover:** Elnur/Shutterstock; Len Green/Shutterstock; **p6:** MIXA/Shutterstock; **p7t:** Shioguchi; **p7cl:** Africa Studio/Shutterstock; **p7cr:** OUP; **p7bl:** Pilipphoto/Shutterstock; **p7br:** Mika/Corbis; **p8t:** Luis Enrique Ascui/Reuters/Corbis; **p8b:** Blue Jean Images/Getty Images; **p9r:** Ken McKay/Rex; **p9l:** Andersen Ross/Getty Images; **p10:** Pictorial Press Ltd/Alamy; **p12:** Monique Pietri/akg-images; **p13:** Keren Su/Corbis; **p14t:** Issouf Sanogo/AFP/Getty Images; **p14b:** Jacob Silberberg/Getty Images; **p15t:** DeAgostini/Getty Images; **p15c:** Michael Harder/Alamy; **p15b:** Africa Media Online/akg-images; **p16:** Sanjeev Gupta/epa/Corbis; **p17t:** photosindia.com; **p17b:** Lawrence JC Baron/Demotix; **p19:** © Agencia Brasil/Alamy; **p20:** MIXA/Shutterstock; **p21t:** Archivist/Alamy; **p21b:** Penny Hillcrest/Shutterstock; **p22:** akg-images; **p23t:** Dance by Beytan/Alamy; **p23b:** Pictorial Press Ltd/Alamy; **p24t:** Gail Mooney/Corbis; **p24b:** Ria Nowost/akg-images; **p25t:** Andreas Solaro/AFP/Getty Images; **p25b:** Bettmann/Corbis; **p26t:** Richard Levine/Demotix/Corbis; **p26b:** James Brunker UK/Alamy; p27t: akg-images; **p27b:** OUP; **p28t:** Michael Ochs Archives/Getty Images; **p28b:** Planet News Archive/SSPL/Getty Images; **p29t:** Stephan Hoerold/Getty Images; **p29b:** Alfred Wekelo/Shutterstock; **p31:** PYMCA/Alamy; **p32:** Disderi/Corbis; **p33:** Robbie Jack/Corbis; **p34l:** The Print Collector/Alamy; **p34r:** Hulton-Deutsch Collection/Corbis; **p35:** Alastair Muir/Rex; **p36:** age fotostock Spain, S.L./Alamy; **p37:** Michael Heimlich/Shutterstock; Backgrounds; Curly Pat/Shutterstock; GarryKillian/Shutterstock; TashaNatasha/Shutterstock; troyka/Shutterstock; RLN/Shutterstock; New Line/Shutterstock; Goldenarts/Shutterstock; De-V/Shutterstock; newcorner/Shutterstock; MaryMo/Shutterstock; Noppanun K/Shutterstock; MT511/Shutterstock

Houghton Mifflin Harcourt Publishing Company
125 High Street
Boston, MA 02110
www.hmhco.com

Contents

The Amazing World of Dance 4
Why Dance? 6
What Dancers Wear 8
The Thrill of Performance 10
The First Steps 12
Discovering African Dance 14
Postcards from India 16
Latin Dance – Time to Party! 18
Flamenco – A Romani Tale 20
May I Have This Dance? 22
European Folk Dancing 24
Folk Dancing in the British Isles 26
Dancing in the U.S. 28
Street Dance Goes Global 30
Ballet 32
The Dancing Rebels 34
Dancing into the Future 36
Glossary 38
Index 39

The Amazing World Of Dance

We're going to take you on a breath-taking journey into the wonderful world of dance. You'll understand how important dance has been to humans throughout history.

You'll travel back in time and to faraway places. You'll visit theatres, temples, and city streets. You'll learn about the human body, different cultures, music, and costumes.

There are many more styles out there than we can cover in these pages. Use this book to begin exploring the world of dance for yourself.

Your dancing body

Artists have their paintbrushes and musicians have their instruments, but dancers have the most exciting tool of all: the human body.

Your body can ...

JUMP in the AIR

SPIN AROUND

STAMP and CLAP

and a whole lot more.

You can move quickly or slowly. You can travel across the floor or turn around on the spot. You can move with others or on your own. The combinations of moves and shapes you can make are endless.

Soon you're going to collect your ticket for a dance world tour. But before then, let's get warmed up!

Why Dance?

Dancing is a fun way to keep fit and healthy.

Strengthens your muscles and bones.

Increases the flexibility of your joints and muscles.

Helps maintain a healthy weight.

Improves your coordination and balance.

Improves your fitness.

If you want to dance well, you need to look after your body.

Here are some top tips …

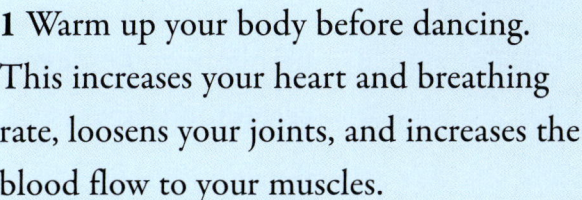

1 Warm up your body before dancing. This increases your heart and breathing rate, loosens your joints, and increases the blood flow to your muscles.

2 Get enough sleep.

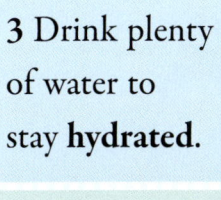

3 Drink plenty of water to stay **hydrated**.

4 Choose more healthy foods …

5 … and fewer unhealthy foods.

Dance isn't just good for your body, it's good for your mind as well. When you dance, your brain releases chemicals called endorphins (*say* en-dor-fins).

Endorphins help you feel happier. Dancing also helps improve concentration and reduce stress levels, and can improve self-confidence.

What Dancers Wear

✱ Look at how this ballroom dancer's dress swirls as she turns.

Costume is a hugely important part of most dance styles. It helps highlight and exaggerate certain movements, and is sometimes part of the dance itself.

In China, women wear dresses with long silk sleeves which they whirl around them to exaggerate the movements of the arms and hands. This costume style goes back to ancient times.

In Kabuki (*say* ka-boo-key), a form of dance-drama from Japan, elaborate versions of traditional Japanese **kimonos** are often worn.

Costumes can help dancers portray a particular character, provide added visual elements or reflect the mood of the dance.

Practice clothing

For classes and rehearsals, dancers wear comfortable layers of clothes to keep their muscles warm and allow them to move easily. These can be taken off or put on as they warm up and cool down. Dancers wear a mix of layers for class. These can include:

* leotard
* tights
* vest top
* cardigan
* t-shirt/long-sleeved top
* shorts
* tracksuit pants
* leg warmers.

The Thrill of Performance

Dance classes help dancers to learn complicated steps and movements, but these are only a part of being a great dancer.

Great dancers are fascinating to watch because they:

* perform movements with feeling
* bring a character to life
* make a strong connection with other dancers and with the audience.

* When ballet dancer Anna Pavlova performed the role of The Dying Swan in 1905, audiences across the world were moved to tears.

The power of music

Music helps shape a dance. Dance styles are often linked to a particular style of music.

classical music — tap dance
jazz music — ballet
hip-hop — street dance

Dancers count the beats of the music as they learn a dance. This helps them perform the right movement at the right time.

The mood of a piece of music affects the way a dancer performs the steps. It helps the dancer express different emotions in their movements.

Rhythm: a regular pattern of beats. The rhythm of the music affects the timing of the steps.

Tempo: the speed of the music. The tempo of the music affects the speed of the dance.

This is your ticket for an unforgettable journey. Get set to go on a dance world tour!

The First Steps

The story of dance is the story of human history.

Although the date we started dancing will never be known, some say that as soon as early humans could walk and talk, they danced.

Dance in early times was part of ancient **rituals** and social events. It is possible that dance was also used to pass stories from one generation to another. People lived in tribes in many parts of the world and each tribe would have its own dances and traditions. Over generations some of these evolved into the tribal and folk dances you can still see in the world today.

This means we have been dancing for 1.5 million years or more!

✷ Cave paintings in the Bhimbetka Rock Shelters in India are possibly the oldest known record of dancing in the world. They date back approximately 9,000 years.

All about African dance

* Rhythm is the most important part of African music and dance. Singing, drumming, clapping the hands, and stamping the feet all create the rhythms of the dance.

* Dances are frequently performed in large groups with onlookers joining in.

* Dance is for everybody, old and young.

* Dance in Africa is used to celebrate, to heal, and to mark important stages in life.

★ In the Adumu dance, young **Maasai** warriors competitively jump up and down, their heels not touching the floor. Others stand in a circle and sing, their voices getting higher with the jumps.

Discovering African Dance

Many of Africa's groups and tribes developed their own dances and still perform them today. Here's a taste of a few ...

Guinea

The Moribayassa (*say* mor-ee-bi-yassa) is a celebration of life, performed by a woman who has overcome hard times. The dance traditionally starts and ends at a mango tree.

Ghana

Kpanlogo (*say* pan-logo) is a fun, lively dance performed to drums that began in the 1960s in Ghana's capital city, Accra.

Egypt

Raqs Sharqi (*say* racks shark-ee) features **undulating** movements of the hips and **torso**. The rules of Islam did not allow men and women to dance together and the **origins** of Raqs Sharqi lie in the ancient dances women used to perform for each other.

South Africa, Zulu region

One of the most famous Zulu (*say* zoo-loo) dances is the Indlamu (*say* ind-thla-mu) War Dance, usually performed by men to drumming. It features repeated high kicks with the legs brought down sharply and slammed into the floor.

Xhosa region of South East Africa

The Umteyo Shaking Dance is performed by young Xhosa (*say* ko-sa) men. It involves rapid shaking of the chest so that the whole spine seems to be rippling.

Postcards from India

India is a country of mountains and deserts, lively colors and spices, rich history and traditions. Its different dance styles reflect this vibrant mix.

Indian classical dance

Indian classical dance is linked to the country's ancient Hindu religion. The most famous style is Bharatanatyam (*say* ba-rat-a-nat-yam), developed over 2,000 years ago in the temples of southern India. Bharatanatyam features beautiful poses, hand gestures, and foot movements performed with a group of seated live musicians. The dance features over 50 single-handed and double-handed gestures, each with a different meaning.

Bhangra

Bhangra was originally a folk dance performed by men in northern India to celebrate the harvest. Today, Bhangra is a hugely popular style of music and a dance full of energy, joy, and color. Danced at weddings, festivals, and parties all over the world, it features energetic jumping, hopping, and arm gestures, often to the beats of the dhol (*say* dole) drum.

Bollywood dance

Bollywood dance is a mixture of Indian classical and folk dance, Western jazz and street dance, Latin dance, and Arabic dance. It came from India's Bollywood films, which feature spectacular song-and-dance numbers.

With catchy music, bright costumes and large groups of dancers who perform anywhere from sandy beaches to crowded city streets, these dances are the highlight of many movies!

Latin Dance – Time to Party!

Latin dance comes from Latin America and the Caribbean.

Latin dances can be fun, like the Salsa and Cha Cha Cha, or dramatic like the Tango. Their history is a multicultural one. Take a look at the influences that have shaped this dance style.

1 The dances of local tribes like the Aztecs and Incas.

2 Folk and country dances from Europeans, particularly the Spanish and Portuguese, who colonized Latin America from the 1600s onwards.

3 African dance brought by people who were enslaved by Spanish and Portuguese planters to grow sugar.

Carnival time!

Latin dances are popular all over the world and are performed at festivals, in dance clubs, and at dance competitions. Latin music is usually played by a large band of musicians. Guitars and percussion instruments such as drums and maracas are commonly used.

Latin music is often happy and upbeat, but for some dances it is more dramatic.

The most thrilling celebration of Latin dance in the world!

Carnival in Rio de Janeiro

Dancers and bands from up to 200 Samba schools. Five days to watch, listen, and party with over two million people. Dazzling costumes! Spectacular floats! Fantastic music!

Flamenco – A Gypsy Tale

Flamenco is more than a Spanish dance style – it's a passionate mix of song, dance, and guitar accompanied by rhythmic clapping called "palmas."

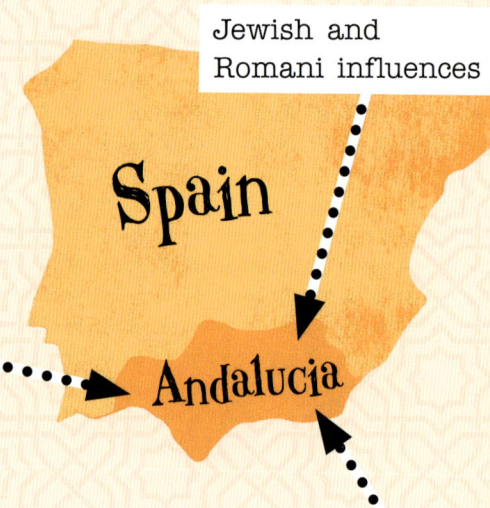

Jewish and Romani influences

Latin American influences

Arab and Moorish influences

Flamenco developed in the nineteenth century, but the roots of flamenco are full of mystery. This is because the dance was created by groups of people who didn't write their stories down.

One of the most popular theories is that flamenco began in the 1400s when **Romanies** arrived from India in Andalucia (*say* An-da-loo-thia), Spain. They lived in the mountains, along with Jewish people and **Moorish** people. Over time, these different cultures combined with local Andalucian folk song and dance, and influences from Latin America, to make flamenco!

Dressing to dance flamenco

Today's female flamenco dancers wear colorful ruffled dresses. These developed from the simple dresses worn by Romani and local peasant women in the 1800s.

Flamenco shoes have nails in the soles and heels. Nowadays, they help the dancers' feet stamp out rhythms, but when flamenco began it was performed outdoors and these nails helped the dancers' shoes grip the bare earth.

May I Have This Dance?

During the eighteenth century, social dancing in Europe was divided into two types.

Country or folk dances were performed by poorer people living in the countryside to mark community and family celebrations.

Europe

Ballroom dances were performed by the upper classes at parties and events. In the 18th and 19th century, grand balls were one of the only ways in which men and women could meet.

Ballroom dances today are usually performed "in hold" like this.

Invitation to the grand ball 1815

There are strict rules on male and female behavior at the ball. Dances must be performed in small groups or by men and women dancing side by side. No dancing "in hold" is allowed.

Dancing "in hold" was considered very daring when it was first seen in the early 1800s.

Today's ballroom dancing no longer takes place in private houses but in competitions all over the world where couples compete for prizes.

✱ 1930s films starring Fred Astaire and Ginger Rogers made ballroom dancing glamorous.

European Folk Dancing

Many early ballroom dances, including the polka and mazurka, developed from European folk dances.

Hopak (*say* hoe-pack) or Cossack Dance

An athletic dance that began among horse-riding male **Cossack** warriors; it involves lots of jumps and squats.

From: Ukraine and southern Russia
Performed: By warriors to celebrate after a battle
Top Move: Squat kicks and split jumps
Strength: 10
Difficulty: 10
Energy: 10

Kalamatianos (*say* kah-lah-mah-tee-ah-nohs) or Handkerchief Dance

Dancers hold hands in a line and perform sideways steps in a slow-quick-quick rhythm. The lead dancer often dances with a handkerchief.

From: Greece
Performed: Weddings and other celebrations
Top Move: Criss-crossing footwork
Strength: 2
Difficulty: 3
Energy: 4

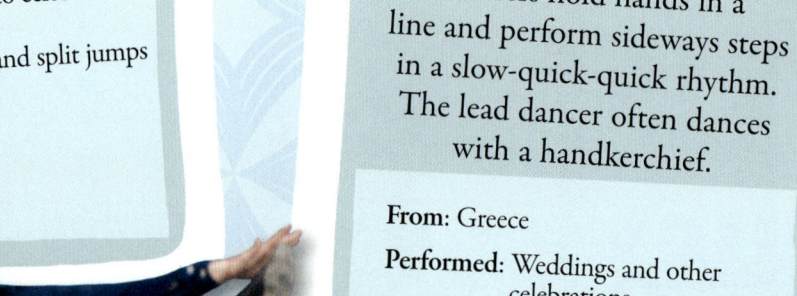

Folk dances took place as part of community and family celebrations in the countryside. Each country or region has its own unique dances, traditional music, and costumes.

Schuhplattler (*say shoo-plat-ler*) or Slap Dance

A powerful male dance in which men stomp their feet, jump, and slap the soles of their shoes with their hands.

From: Bavaria, Germany, and Alpine areas of Austria
Performed: As a **courtship** dance
Top Move: Foot slapping
Strength: 5
Difficulty: 8
Energy: 8

Tarantella (*say tar-an-tell-a*)

An energetic folk dance which features rapid whirling and light, quick steps.

From: Southern Italy
Performed: Traditional Italian weddings.
Top Move: Whirling and turning
Strength: 3
Difficulty: 6
Energy: 6

Folk Dancing in the British Isles

People have danced in Britain and Ireland for hundreds of years. Take a look!

Irish step dancing

Long ago, Irish dancing was taught by traveling dance masters in kitchens and farm buildings. There wasn't much room to move, and some say this is why the arms and body are kept very still – even though the feet and legs move very fast!

Welsh clog dancing

This used to be danced by men to show how fit and athletic they were. Their wooden clogs would strike out rhythms on the floor. They would also perform tricks such as putting out a candle with their feet!

Scottish Highland dancing

Highland dancing is so athletic it is recognized as a sport. The most famous Highland dance is the Sword Dance, which is performed over two crossed swords.

In one dance, called a Highland Fling, a dancer jumps vertically 196 times in less than two minutes!

British Isles

English morris dancing

Imagine dancing with bells, sticks, and handkerchiefs! These props are part of morris dances, which have been performed during festivals in English villages since the 1400s.

Immigrants brought British clog and Irish step dancing to the U.S. in the eighteenth and nineteenth centuries. Tap dance developed in the U.S. from a combination of these dances and those from enslaved people from West Africa.

Dancing in the U.S.

Dance styles brought over by enslaved African people
+ dance traditions of European immigrants
= tap, jazz, and street dance

Tap dance

Tap dance has a long history but became popular in the 1920s thanks to performers in traveling stage shows and later, in the 1930s, in Hollywood movies.

✲ Bill "Bojangles" Robinson was one of the first famous tap dancers.

Jazz dance

Jazz dance developed over a hundred years ago in New York and other big cities in the United States. It was very popular in clubs. Later, influenced by ballet and contemporary dance, it was performed in **Broadway** and Hollywood musicals like *Chicago* and *A Chorus Line*.

✲ Daring Jazz dances thrilled young women in 1920s New York.

28

Everybody dance!

Social dancing took on a new meaning in the 1970s and 1980s – anyone could jump on a dance floor and have a good time!

The sharp movements of body parts like ribs, shoulders, and hips in jazz and street dance come from African dance, where different parts of the body move to different rhythms at the same time.

1870-1900

1650-1860

1970s – Disco

Disco music was a huge trend in New York nightclubs in the early 1970s. Basic disco moves are simple steps and turns. Hips move side to side, arms rotate, and fingers point – all to the beat of some funky disco tunes!

1980s – American line dancing

Dressed in cowboy hats and boots, dancers stand in lines and perform **synchronized** steps forwards, backwards, and sideways to country music. Line dancing's roots come from the Country and Western dance style of the American Midwest. Yee-haw!

Street Dance Goes Global

Touch down in the United States of America to discover how street dance has taken over the world!

USA

June 1974

Today I was hanging out on a street corner in New York's South Bronx neighborhood with a bunch of other kids. We were listening to a DJ playing hip-hop beats.

One by one, the boys stood up and **improvised** moves on the sidewalk. They competed with each other in battles, outdoing each other with faster and faster moves. I had met some of the first breakdancers!

Street dance timeline

1970s
Street dance is the name given to improvised dance styles like breakdance. These developed in black and Latin American communities on the streets of New York and the West Coast.

1980s
Performers start to mix street styles, such as popping and locking, with jazz dance in their music videos.

1990s
Choreographers and trained dancers in America begin to mix street dance with jazz, ballet, and contemporary dance. This new style of street dance, which was taught in studios, gave dancers steps to follow, instead of them making up their own as they performed.

2000s
Street dance is made popular by television. It's seen everywhere from music videos to TV talent shows. Street dance is performed in theater shows for the first time. There are now thousands of **amateur** and professional street dance crews across the world!

Ballet: A World of Wonder and Determination

Ballet began in fifteenth-century Italy, but became the art form we know today in France.

The French King Louis XIV set up the first ballet school in 1661. Ballet dancers make it look easy, but it requires years of hard work and training to become a professional ballet dancer.

France

Italy

Dancing on the tips of your toes is called *en pointe*, and it isn't easy ... Dancers must protect their toes with pads or tape to prevent painful blisters. A Principal Dancer can wear out three pairs of pointe shoes in a single performance!

✶ Marie Taglioni was one of ballet's first female stars. In 1832, she was the first dancer to dance *en pointe*.

The most famous ballets were created in the nineteenth century. Ballets such as *Swan Lake* and *The Nutcracker* feature fairytale-like stories and soaring classical music, and transport audiences to an enchanted world.

Who's who?

In a ballet **company**, dancers belong to a **rank**.

Corps de ballet: dancers who dance together as a group.

Coryphée (*say* coree-fay): a leading dancer in a *corps de ballet*, may dance small group roles and solos.

Soloist: dances solo roles and sometimes is an **understudy** for principal dancers.

Principal Dancer: the star who performs a lead role.

Ballet steps and positions all have French names. This means a dancer can take a class anywhere in the world, even if they don't understand the local language.

corps de ballet

soloist

The Dancing Rebels: Modern Dance

In the early twentieth century in North America, some dancers were fed up with the strict rules of ballet.

They wanted to express themselves more freely. These dancers helped create modern dance, which is studied and performed all over the world. Let's meet some of these dancing rebels ...

USA

FACT FILE

Name: Isadora Duncan

Lived: 1877–1927

Rebel Rating: 10

Shocked and inspired audiences with her natural, barefoot dancing, and her free-flowing clothing.

FACT FILE

Name: Martha Graham

Lived: 1894–1991

Rebel rating: 9

Her dance works featured strong female characters and a way of moving the body from the "center" in the lower stomach which had never been seen before.

FACT FILE

Name: Merce Cunningham

Lived: 1919–2009

Rebel rating: 8

Choreographed dances using chance procedures like tossing a coin. Created dances performed in silence or where music was added after they were created.

Dance feature	Classical ballet	Modern dance
Costume	Tutus and detailed costumes.	Simple costumes.
Feet	Pointed, wearing special shoes.	Pointed or flexed at the ankle, bare feet.
Movements	Specific range of steps and positions. Controlled and graceful. Performed standing.	Much freer range of movements. Performed on the floor, standing, and anywhere in between.
Themes	Tells a story.	Based on a theme, thought, or idea.
Music	Classical.	Any kind of music, sound, or silence!

Dancing into the Future

On our dance world tour, we have explored this amazing art form from the beginnings of human civilization to modern street dance crews.

Have you noticed how dance never stops developing and changing? As humans travel around the world, they take their dances with them. Over the years, these mix together to create brand new dance styles.

Today we live in a world where different cultures live side by side, travel is easy, and trends spread across the Internet. Maybe, in the future, it will be technology that creates the next big dance revolution?

As dancers, choreographers, scientists, and programmers work together, the creative possibilities are endless.

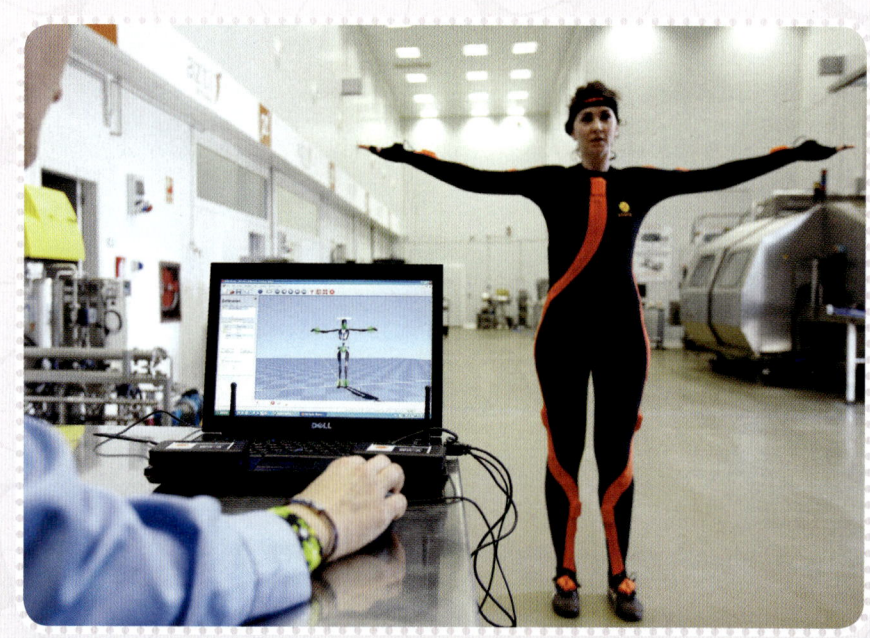

✱ Motion capture uses human movement to bring characters to life in video games and animations.

Social media allows mass public dances called "flash mobs" to be organized and new dance crazes to spread worldwide in days.

We don't know how and where we'll experience dance in the next 100 years, but the Internet, social media, and TV shows have brought dance into people's homes. More and more dance is performed away from the stage – on city streets, in parks, and at the beach – turning the whole world into a theater!

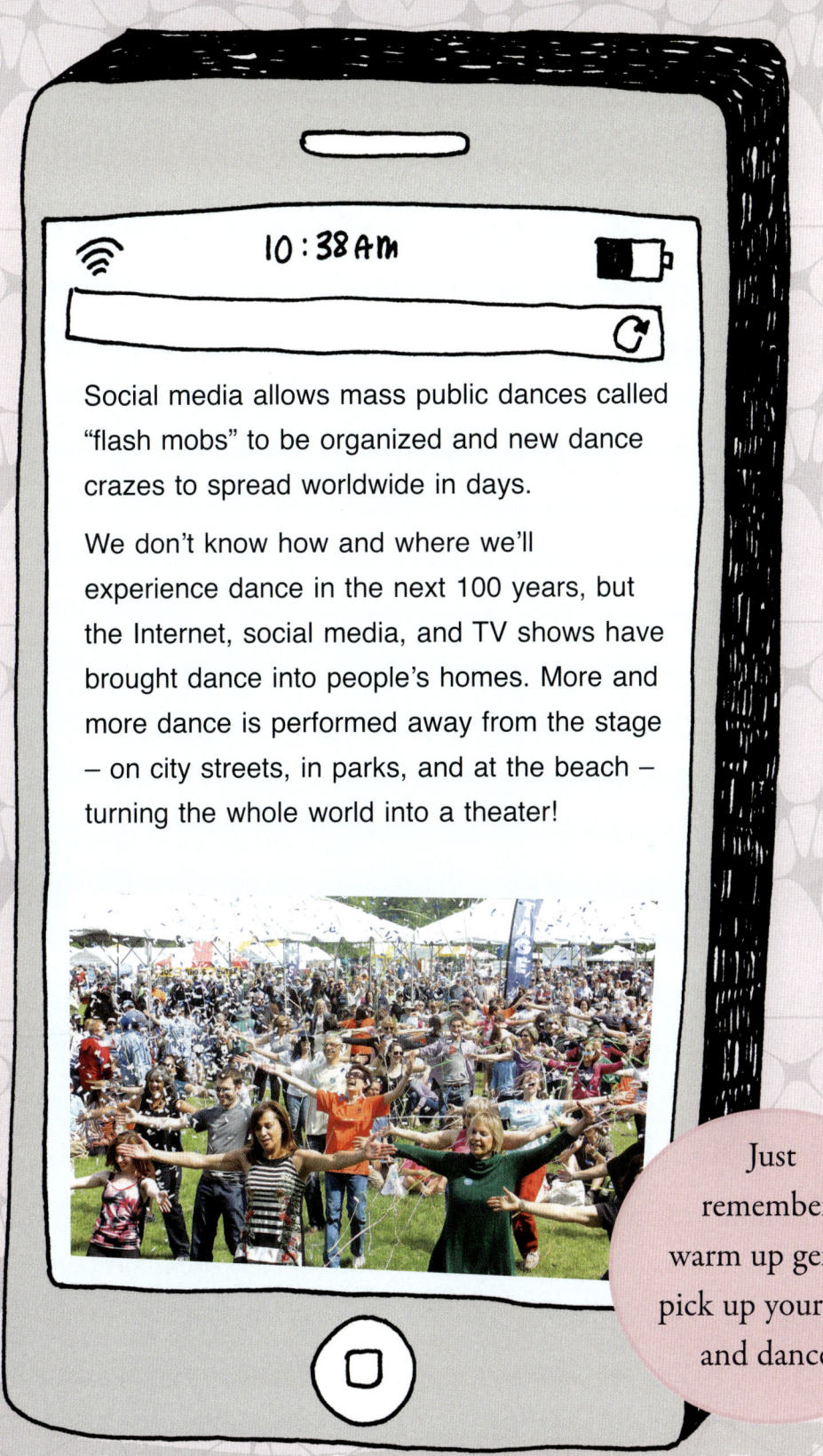

Just remember: warm up gently, pick up your feet, and dance!

Glossary

amateur: someone who takes part in an activity without being paid, as a hobby or for fun

Broadway: an area in New York known for its many theaters

choreographers: people who decide the sequence of steps in a dance

company: group of dancers who perform together

Cossack: a member of a group of warrior people from Ukraine and Southern Russia, famous for their horseriding skills

courtship: the beginning of a romantic relationship

hydrated: having enough water in your body

immigrants: people who come to live permanently in a foreign country

improvised: made up as you go along, without any rehearsal or preparation

kimonos: a long, loose traditional Japanese robe with wide sleeves

Maasai: a group of people from East Africa

Moorish: belonging to a group of medieval Muslim people from North Africa, who settled in Spain

origins: the start of something

rank: a group of ballet dancers who have the same level of skill

rituals: sequences of actions or activities which are performed in a particular way and on particular occasions

Romani: a group of people who live in caravans or similar vehicles, and travel from place to place

synchronized: happening at the same time

torso: the main part of the human body – not the head, arms, or legs

understudy: a person who learns a role in case the main performer is unable to perform

undulating: moving in a smooth, wave-like way

Index

African dances 13–15
ancient dance 12
ballroom dance 22–23
benefits of dance 6–7
Bollywood 17
breakdance 30–31
clothing 8–9, 21, 29, 34–35
corps de ballet 33
disco dance 29
famous dancers 23, 28, 31, 32, 34–35
flash mobs 37
folk dances 22, 24–27
instruments 5, 14–15, 16–17, 19, 20
jazz dance 28
line dancing 29
music videos 31
music 11, 17, 19, 29, 30, 33, 35
principal dancer 32–33
Rio carnival 19
shoes 21, 25, 26, 32, 35
tap dance 28

About the Author

My life-long passion for dance began as a child in my local library where I read dozens of books about dancers, dance technique, and history. Along with attending dance classes, one of my favorite things was choreographing dance shows in the garden.

I studied at Trinity Laban Conservatoire of Music and Dance, and have been a Director and Producer for many different dance companies, organizing lots of events to get more people dancing. I still love reading books about dance, and now I write them too!